D0555790

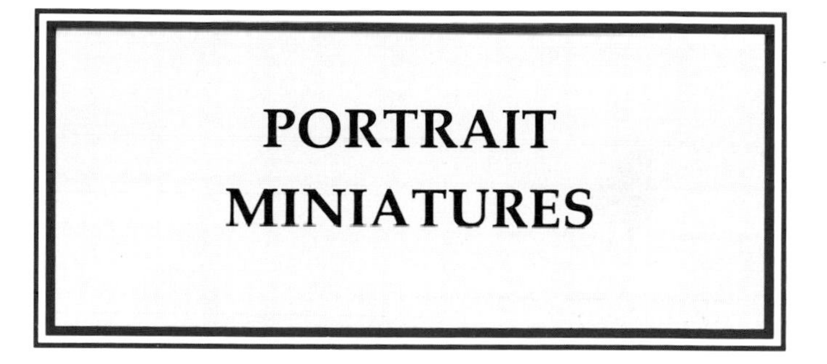
PORTRAIT
MINIATURES

Dat

PORTRAIT MINIATURES

STEPHEN BUTLER

Picture selection by
Julia Brown

STUDIO EDITIONS
LONDON

Cover: The Earl of Pembroke,
Peter Oliver (c. *1594–1647).*

Frontispiece: Young Man Against a Tree,
Nicholas Hilliard (1547–1619).

This edition published 1994 by
Studio Editions Ltd
Princess House, 50 Eastcastle Street
London, W1N 7AP, England

Design by Michael R Carter
Printed and bound in Singapore

ISBN 1 85891 180 X

INTRODUCTION

The great age of the portrait miniature came early in its history, in the sixteenth century. For the most part since then, miniatures have been unfairly regarded as merely reflecting the successive changes affecting painting as a whole. Few miniaturists achieved lasting fame. Only one, the Elizabethan Nicholas Hilliard, is now widely known, but there have been many others of great talent and vision.

The portrait miniature was the invention of a single man, Jean Clouet (*d. c.* 1540), Court Painter to François I of France. He made a number of small, portable portraits in watercolour on vellum (parchment) stretched over card. The idea spread only gradually, becoming established not in France but in the Low Countries and then in England. Popularized at Henry VIII's court by Lucas Hornebolte and Hans Holbein, miniature painting or 'limning' became, at the court of Elizabeth I, a distinct and highly fashionable art form, with a set of aesthetic values quite separate from those of conventional portraiture.

The vogue for miniatures at Elizabeth's court is not hard to explain, nor are the reasons for its gradual decline thereafter. The form lent itself best to portraiture, and therein lay both its strength and its chief weakness. Portraiture in the Middle Ages had been as much symbolic as representational, so to have a small, portable and above all accurate image was an enormous boon. Minia-

Portrait of a Dowager, *François Clouet* (d. *1672*). *François was the son of the originator of the portrait miniature, Jean Clouet. His very rare but excellent miniatures may have influenced the genre's popularity in the Low Countries and England.*

tures could be presented to visiting dignitaries, or sent abroad with ambassadors, much more easily than conventional portraits, and Hilliard's many miniatures of Elizabeth fulfilled a political role in propagandizing the splendours of her court.

Miniatures were often framed or encased in highly wrought, precious metalwork, encrusted with pearls and jewels, so increasing the image's aura of preciousness. They were therefore valued not only as political symbols, but also as tokens of love and desire in an age which idealized courtly love and made a cult of secrecy and intrigue. Easily hidden yet beautiful and luxurious, the miniature became a favourite expression of devotion among an immensely wealthy aristocracy, not least because with both men and women vying to outshine each other in the finery of their clothes, hairstyles and jewellery, limning was the perfect expression of their glamour.

Part of the popularity of the miniature lay in the ability of Hilliard and his followers to maintain a distance from conventional painting. This was to some extent an inherited perception, for limning was originally not a branch of full-scale painting but a parallel development. Clouet's inspiration had been to combine the skills of Burgundian manuscript illumination with those of portraiture on medallions, seals and coins. Large-scale easel-painting barely existed in his world. The decorative richness of the manuscript tradition is one ancestor of the dazzling colour and ornament of the Elizabethan miniature, but with the decline of monastic influence, these origins were gradually forgotten, as painting took over from illumination as the pre-eminent visual art. Even Clouet's work displays little formal resemblance to illumination despite similarities of technique, and we find, very soon after Hilliard's day, that the limner was regarded simply as a painter who worked – or copied – on a small scale, and whose works were expected to resemble conventional paintings. Thus miniature painting lost any chance of developing a unique language. Its scale came to be seen as a limitation despite the efforts of a few artists to broaden its subject-matter.

Miniatures were originally produced in translucent watercolour and opaque bodycolour on vellum. After about 1600 oil paint was sometimes used, but this never achieved the luminosity which is central to the miniature's appeal. As miniatures became more highly valued, the card on which the vellum was mounted was replaced by ivory since this was less inclined to warp, apart from being more valuable. The Venetian artist Rosalba Carriera discovered that painting directly on to ivory gave exceptional smoothness but still allowed the light to shine through.

The perceived link between limning and easel-painting meant that miniatures closely followed the changing fortunes of art as a whole from the seventeenth century onwards. The great court

Opposite: Richard Sackville, 3rd Earl of Dorset, *Isaac Oliver (1565-1617). In a development of Hilliard's 'cabinet miniature' full-length portraits. Oliver's masterpiece is a tour-de-force of colour, pattern and texture.*

Sir Thomas Gresley, *Nicholas Hilliard (1547–1619). The Gresley Jewel, as this double portrait locket is known, was commissioned to celebrate Sir Thomas's wedding to Catherine Walsingham.*

Christian Frederick Zincke, *William Hoare (1752). The limner's enormous technical control is well illustrated in this lively drawing of the Dresden-born Zincke, who enjoyed a long and successful career in England. Note that he is using a fine nib rather than a brush.*

painters such as Rubens and Van Dyck are paralleled by fine miniaturists; and as English portraiture declined after the death of Charles II so did the standard of limning.

The second great age of the miniature, from about 1750 to 1850, reflected the Georgian revival of court painting in England under the influence of Reynolds and Gainsborough. The contemporary school of miniature painting shares their panache and elegance. George Engleheart and Richard

Cosway were among the leading miniaturists, and indeed the leading artists of their day. In France, portraiture and small-scale copies of Old Masters, religious and historical subjects had become well-established in the Baroque age, which also saw the rise of erotic art in miniature. The Neo-Classical style which evolved in post-Revolutionary France was also eminently suited to the miniature in its combination of simplicity of line and form with exact description. Artists such as Jean-Urbain Guérin and Jean-Baptiste Isabey enjoyed international reputations which deserve to be revived.

The advent of photography meant that mainstream painting turned to challenging traditional visual logic and modes of representation, and miniaturists increasingly lacked academic and critical attention. Yet there is no reason why the restrictions of the form should not provide both a technical challenge and the opportunity for innovative expression. In the meantime limners have left us with some of the most beautiful and delicate of all paintings, and five centuries' accumulation of imagery lies largely forgotten, waiting to be rediscovered.

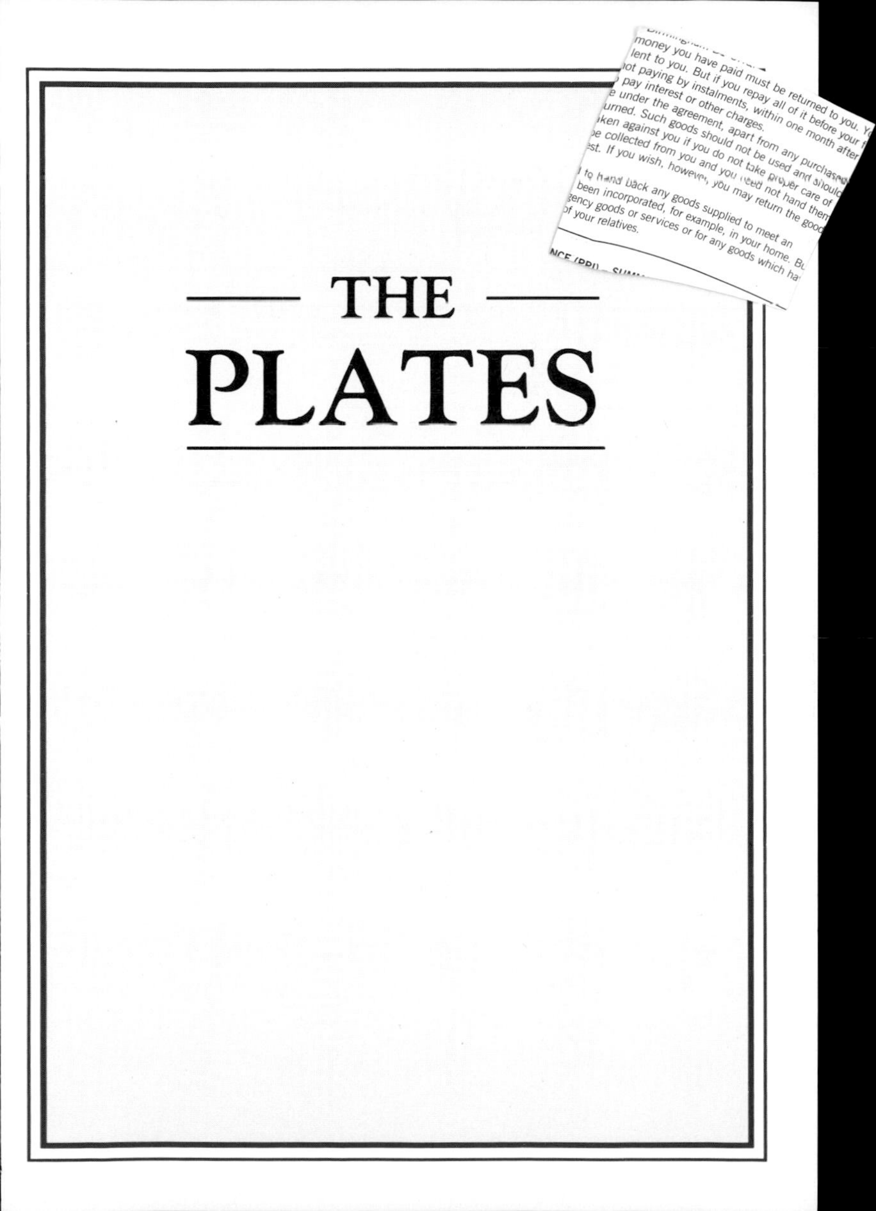

THE PLATES

PLATE 1

Lucas Hornebolte (*c*. 1500–44)

Henry VIII

Hornebolte came from a Flemish family, one of many who emigrated to England to escape religious persecution. His sister Susannah was also a painter, who sold at least one painting to the great Albrecht Dürer. There is strong evidence to suggest that it was Lucas who taught Hans Holbein the technique of miniature painting. Hornebolte is known to have been paid for work by Henry VIII in 1525, and he stayed in England until his death, receiving an annual salary from the King of £33 6*s*.

Hornebolte's work is a fairly direct revision of Clouet's technique, though more polished in style. His variety of head-and-shoulders portraiture, with the subject half-face and flatly lit, painted on vellum with a gold inscription, provides the starting-point for a rich vein of English limning.

The inscription can be interpreted as meaning that Henry was thirty-five, or in this thirty-fifth year (i.e. thirty-four) – this accounts for a slight uncertainty in dating the picture.

HK
HR
VIII
O
AN
XXXV
HK

PLATE 2

Hans Holbein the Younger (1497/8–1543)

Mrs Pemberton

Hans Holbein, one of the greatest portraitists of any age, came from Augsburg in Germany, where his father was a painter. He moved to Basle in 1515, becoming a citizen and rapidly acquiring an international reputation. He also travelled in France and Italy before visiting England in 1526. On his return in 1532, he enjoyed a wide variety of commissions from Henry VIII for paintings, jewellery designs and architectural schemes. Having learned the techniques of limning from Lucas Hornebolte, Holbein rapidly surpassed him in ability in the medium, and was sent abroad by Henry to paint miniatures of prospective brides. Holbein's portrait of Anne of Cleves, considered very faithful by contemporaries, persuaded Henry to propose a marriage which was never consummated.

A dozen or so Holbein miniatures survive. *Mrs Pemberton* is among the finest of them, and indeed is one of the greatest of all his works. Dispassionate and utterly simple, this pensive portrait is among the most memorable of the hundreds of miniatures of women which soon followed.

ANNO
·ETATIS·SVÆ·

PLATE 3

Hans Eworth (*c.* 1520–74)

Mary I

Eworth is a mysterious figure, who signed his pictures only with the initials HE. Some scholars argue that he is the artist 'Jan Euworts' recorded in Antwerp in 1540; others maintain that since the form of the HE monogram and the style of painting vary considerably there were at least two artists working concurrently using this signature.

Eworth succeeded Hans Holbein as Court Painter to Henry VIII, and Holbein is the chief influence on the 'HE' paintings and miniatures. Eworth's figures are more formally posed than Holbein's, but are often, as here, slightly ungainly in their attitudes. Nevertheless he was an artist of great skill and observation, and this is a persuasive image depicting a woman of enormous strength of character and determination. This impression is strengthened by the frontal pose and level gaze – even the hands have a certain tension.

PLATE 4

Nicholas Hilliard (1547–1619)

George Clifford, 3rd Earl of Cumberland

The son of a Protestant family from Exeter, Hilliard trained as a goldsmith. About 200 miniatures by him survive, reflecting the great popularity of this type of painting, a fashion he created almost single-handed. Hilliard's talent lay in his jeweller's sense of visual design, and his best-known works are small, densely patterned images, usually head-and-shoulders portraits. He was also the originator of full-length portraits in miniature, as in this fine portrait of the Earl as Queen's Champion. The Earl wears the kind of splendidly extravagant costume for which the Elizabethans could always invent an excuse, such as a masque or pageant. The shield is not a heraldic one, but part of this ensemble, evidently devised for a ceremony with an astronomical theme. Presumably Elizabeth is symbolized by the sun, around which the heavenly bodies of the court revolve.

GEORGE

PLATE 5

Nicholas Hilliard (1547–1619)

Elizabeth I

Hilliard produced at least 15 miniatures of Elizabeth, and no other sitter suited his technique better. The Queen's habitual ornate dress, embroidered with gold thread and coloured silks, encrusted with hundreds of gems and pearls and set off by fantastic ruffs, sleeves and gloves of lace, could be shown to dazzling effect in the compressed space and brilliant colour of Hilliard's limning style. We know from his own writing that he preferred to pose his sitters in the open air, in direct sunlight where the fewest possible shadows were cast, and certainly this image, with its almost hallucinatory detail, suggests this practice. Hilliard's work was central to the projection of Elizabeth's image as the centre of a confident, expansionist and innovative England, the embodiment of both power and virtue.

PLATE 6

Nicholas Hilliard (1547–1619)
Sir Christopher Hatton

Hilliard is associated with polished full-length portraits in miniature such as the *Young Man Amongst Roses* (*see* Frontispiece), but this early essay in the format is a curious and atypical picture in many ways. He is known to have disliked painting indoors and rarely described interiors, so here he may have been overruled by his client. The pose is stiff and very formal, and Hilliard was evidently – at this stage of his career at least no master of perspective. Possibly this is a copy of a full-size work by another painter which Hatton wanted reproduced in miniature – a practice which became common some years later. Hilliard's attempt to transfer the effect of a conventional portrait is otherwise somewhat baffling. The picture is not nearly as large as the cabinet miniatures of his later years, and although packed with detail has none of the assurance and suavity of the artist at his best.

PLATE 7

Isaac Oliver (*c.* 1565–1617)

An Unknown Man, 26 Years of Age

Isaac Oliver was probably born in Geneva, where his father Pierre, a Huguenot refugee, set up as a goldsmith. Nicholas Hilliard studied there, and when the Oliver family came to England in about 1568, the acquaintance was renewed. Isaac was apprenticed to Hilliard in about 1580, and later in life succeeded him as the preeminent limner of the court.

This picture is typical of the standard head-and-shoulders miniature which was essentially Hilliard's invention, with its bright colour, flat lighting, smooth complexion and extravagant gilding. Oliver was in fact a highly individual artist, able to work in a number of styles, but at this point in his career he was evidently still required to produce portraits in the accepted manner. Oliver's work does, however, even at this stage, display a little more shadowed modelling than his master's, and this became progressively more pronounced in later years. Isaac's son Peter also became a limner, as did Hilliard's son Lawrence, though neither equalled his father's achievements.

Ano Dni 1593
Ætatis Suæ 26

PLATE 8

Isaac Oliver (*c*. 1565–1617)

A Lady, called Frances Howard, Countess of Essex and Somerset

This is one of a pair of images, both about five inches across, about which much scholarly argument has taken place. As the title implies, the identification is not definite, nor has the elaborate costume been explained beyond doubt. The leading theory is that this is Frances Howard in the costume she wore for the masque *Hymenaei*, produced to celebrate her marriage to the Earl of Essex in 1606.

The masque was one of the central artistic activities of the Elizabethan age, combining drama, music, poetry, pantomime, costume and scenery, all specially commissioned from the leading talents of the day, and in which the participants were at once actors and spectators.

The large scale has given Oliver the opportunity for a bravura display of technical prowess, combining extreme detail in the elaboration of the dress and jewels, with a quasi-symmetrical structure which is perhaps intended to accentuate the costume's artificiality.

PLATE 9

Isaac Oliver (*c.* 1565–1617)

Two Girls, aged five and four

These two children's portraits are among Oliver's best-known works, images which are refreshing to modern eyes because of their straightforward, unsentimental handling. Perhaps because he regarded this commission as a break from the conventions of court portraiture, Oliver has adapted the standard format subtly to suit his subjects. They fill the picture surface almost completely, are posed full-face rather than slightly turned, and they are shown half-length rather than head-and-shoulders. Oliver's handling of the detail of needlework and lace is among the finest in any miniature, and the slight variation between the two poses and expressions is a masterstroke of restraint which makes the pair a single work of art. The faces are firmly modelled in the softer, *sfumato* Continental style of which Hilliard would certainly have disapproved. Oliver, however, had made it the fashion by the time James I appointed him royal limner.

PLATE 10

Isaac Oliver (*c*. 1565–1617)

Portrait of a Young Man Seated beneath a Tree

This singular work appears at first glance to resemble a manuscript illumination rather than a miniature. Here Oliver re-works the cabinet miniature format, but unlike Hilliard's work this does not really resemble the full-scale paintings of the day. The background has been geometrically organized and the perspective flattened, and with even distant details in sharp focus, the effect is like the 'carpet' patterning of medieval manuscript painting. However, the scenery is late Renaissance rather than medieval – a chateau and garden, probably invented, combining Classical and jubilantly Baroque features. Enormous care has been taken over the foreground, and the pose, which is a difficult one to bring off even in a large painting, is relaxed and well-balanced. Here again Oliver shows himself to be a stylistic chameleon, capable of much stronger modelling than in the *Unknown Man, 26 Years of Age* (*see* Plate 7).

PLATE 11

Peter Oliver (*c.* 1594–1647)

Venetia Stanley, later Lady Digby

One of the best of the second generation of English miniaturists, Isaac Oliver's son Peter enjoyed considerable success at the court of Charles I, and was a consummate technician, though he lacked his father's adventurous approach. Peter Oliver and his contemporary, Lawrence Hilliard, seem to have produced less work than their fathers, probably because of a swing in taste towards easel-painting in the Dutch grand manner of Rubens and Van Dyck. Increasingly, limners were expected to provide small copies of larger works, and original portrait miniatures began to resemble full-scale pictures in their design. However, this image has a distinctly retrospective flavour and must have been one of the last in the old Hilliardian style.

Venetia Stanley was one of the great beauties of her day. She married Sir Kenelm Digby secretly in 1625, and when she died only eight years later it was rumoured that he had poisoned her. The writer John Aubrey called her the 'most beautiful, desirable' woman, who, 'sanguine and tractable', had several affairs.

PLATE 12

Samuel Cooper (1609–72)
Oliver Cromwell

Samuel Cooper was the pre-eminent genius of the second, naturalistic phase of the portrait miniature. Indeed, his work stands alongside the best of English portraiture of any period. Originally very much in the shadow of his uncle John Hoskins, limner to Charles I, Cooper established his own workshop in about 1642, adapting to the miniature form the lessons of Anthony Van Dyck, who worked at the English court from 1632. His reputation quickly overtook that of Hoskins, and his connections with the court did not prevent Cromwell from sitting for him very soon after the King's execution in 1649.

Cromwell's express instruction was to paint him 'warts and all', and the result is an image of great conviction and immediacy. It is not, as appears, unfinished – this is the working painting from which other, more finished portraits would be done without the sitter being present.

PLATE 13

Bernard Lens (1682–1740)

Portraits of three Girls and a Boy of the Whitmore Family

Bernard Lens was the son and the grandson of limners and his two sons also continued the tradition. His chief importance to English art is that he was the first painter to use ivory as a background to his works, giving them a softer glow and smoother surface. Limner to both George I and George II, Lens cannot be counted an artist of the same level of achievement as Cooper or Oliver. His style reflects the paucity of English art in his time, under the influence of Godfrey Kneller, Principal Painter to George II. While the patterning of the children's clothes is carefully described, the textures are clumsily suggested. A tendency to reduce faces to smooth ovoid shapes and a general stiffness of pose typify the era, although this does give the images a degree of naivety which is appealing.

Lens painted twelve of Sir William Whitmore's children over a fourteen-year period. Here the boy and lowest girl are early – around 1718–20 – and the others date from some ten years later.

PLATE 14

John Smart (*c.* 1741/2–1811)

Self-Portrait

One of the most successful of the numerous good miniaturists working at the end of the eighteenth century, John Smart spent ten years in India as painter to the Nawab of Arcot, returning to London in 1795. His miniatures are noted for their meticulous, 'dry' finish, and while they lack the verve of many of his rivals' work, they are supreme technical achievements. Highlights on the face, for example, are often achieved by leaving bare minute areas of the underlying ivory. He was also a consummate painter of drapery.

It is interesting to speculate whether he was influenced by Moghul miniature painting while in India. Certainly his very bright palette in many works contrasts with the softer, more dissolved colours which were fashionable at the time. He had an extremely high opinion of his own talents, which lost him many friends despite the general admiration for his work.

PLATE 15

Richard Cosway (1742–1821)

Unknown Boy

Born in Tiverton, Devon, and sent to London aged only 11 to study painting, Cosway had a youthful ambition to be a painter of full-scale portraits. Despite a brilliant early career, however, he found little success as an adult and instead turned to miniatures, becoming the best-known of all English eighteenth-century limners.

Renowned as a dandy and womaniser, he was pursued by scandal all his life. Notwithstanding the comparitively free mores of the day, he was regarded as a dangerous libertine, and his marriage was a disaster. He became increasingly unstable, claiming late in life that the Virgin Mary had sat for him.

Despite his social reputation and the consequent hostility of many, Cosway was regarded without peer in his profession. This relaxed, fluent and delicate picture is typical of his output, and in its slight idealization of features, conceptual simplicity and soft opalescent light, typical of English taste at the time.

PLATE 16

George Engleheart (1750–1829)

An Unknown Woman

In Engleheart's best work he displays, as here, an ability to convey character far beyond the usual superficiality of his output. This charming and vivacious portrait captures a glance, rather than a pose; it has both immediacy and depth. Not that it is an entirely naturalistic portrait – the enlarged, very deep blue eyes, for example, are a hallmark of Engleheart's style. However, he has otherwise made little attempt to conventionalize or over-sweeten the features, and the execution of the dress, with its complex creasing and extremely delicate lace trim, is of a very high standard.

Engleheart, one of the youngest of the group of talented English miniaturists active between 1780 and 1820, was arguably the last 'great' exponent of the technique in England, though it continued to flourish in France. Very shortly after his death, the new art of photography began to signal the end of the miniature as a popular form of portrait.

PLATE 17

George Engleheart (1750–1829)

William Howe de Lancey

Of German ancestry, Engleheart studied under Sir Joshua Reynolds and was one of the most productive of all English miniaturists, producing almost 5,000 works in his very long career. His work, not surprisingly, though technically of a very high order, tends to be repetitious and unadventurous in design. He was called upon to produce smooth, somewhat flashy society portraits and that is what he did superbly well. But they are rarely profound character studies, and it is the personality of his sitters, rather than the artist's accomplishment, which occasionally lifts his work above the level of polished mundanity.

William Howe de Lancey is an example of Engleheart's staple professional output, a portrait which, though admirably done, does not really convince us that beyond the peachy complexion, limpid gaze and rosebud lips we may discern anything about the young man himself. Engleheart could produce 200 such images a year; at ten guineas each he had little incentive to do anything more.

PLATE 18

Edward Miles (*c.* 1752–1828)

An Unknown Young Man

Edward Miles first exhibited at the Royal Academy in 1775. Now largely forgotten, he enjoyed an international reputation in his lifetime – and deservedly so, as this superb miniature testifies. An extreme delicacy of touch, exuberant colour and sound drawing ability produce an image which, although perhaps flattering and over-pretty, is wonderfully fresh. The standard of British portraiture was at its highest for a century, and alongside the likes of Reynolds and Ramsay, the miniaturists John Smart, Edward Miles and Ozias Humphrey represent the last great age of the tradition in England.

Indeed, there were so many capable painters and miniaturists working in Britain that a great many sought fame abroad. Some went to America, but Miles travelled first to Russia, in 1797. He probably took with him a recommendation from Queen Charlotte and the Duchess of York, and he worked at the Tsar's court for ten years before retiring to Philadelphia, by which time he was wealthy enough to give up his career.

PLATE 19

Mrs Diana Hill, née Dietz (active 1785–1844)

An Unknown Girl

Diana Dietz, a prizewinning artist as a young woman, was widowed at an early age and emigrated to India, as did many miniaturists, looking for business among the wealthy ruling class of the young colony. The leading artist in Calcutta, where she settled, was Ozias Humphrey; he confessed himself jealous of her abilities and her popularity with clients. She married a soldier, and returned to England on his retirement in 1806.

Apart from the exceptionally pretty Anglo-Indian subject, the reasons for her success are plain to see here. The painting is crisp and assured, the palette well-modulated, the features idealized without being anodyne. While the picture has faults – the too-symmetrical folds of the mob cap, the cupid's bow exaggeration of the lips, the over-simplified curls – the overall effect is very striking. Like so much late-eighteenth-century English portraiture, its charm more than outweighs its somewhat kitsch components.

PLATE 20

Jean-Urbain Guérin (1761–1836)

Georgiana, Duchess of Devonshire and Lady Elizabeth Foster

Guérin was, with Jean-Baptiste Isabey, a leader of the revival of the portrait miniature in France around the time of the Revolution. He came from Strasbourg but worked in Paris from 1785, and his style was much influenced by Roman art, in which there was intense interest due to the discoveries of Pompeii and Herculaneum. Thus, while softly and elegantly painted, the Duchess and her companion are posed in profile in a manner which refers directly to Roman fresco painting.

Guérin was exiled from Paris during the Revolution and it seems likely that this work was created in those years. While miniature painting had been well-established in France for many years, it was decorative painting – often mildly erotic works showing nymphs bathing or playing in gardens – which dominated the form, under the influence of Watteau and Boucher. With the less frivolous atmosphere of the Revolution and the advent of the Neoclassical movement, the portrait miniature came into its own, and enjoyed its greatest period in the Napoleonic era.

PLATE 21

Jean-Baptiste Isabey (1767–1855)

Self-Portrait

The most successful French portrait miniaturist of his day, Isabey was born in Nancy and went to Paris in 1786, where his work attracted the attention of Marie-Antoinette. However, his greatest success came after the Revolution, when Napoleon made him Court Painter. He produced many portraits of Bonaparte, fulfilling much the same role as Hilliard had at the court of Elizabeth I. After the restoration of the monarchy he remained Court Painter, serving three monarchs during his life.

In his official miniatures Isabey could display his technical mastery, but his composition was constrained by tradition. Here he has no such limitations, and has produced a deeply personal work. Melancholy and introspective in atmosphere, it balances this Romanticism with a fashionably sparse Neoclassical setting. It is one of the most striking of all miniature paintings, as effective as any full-size piece.

PLATE 22

Jean-Baptiste Isabey (1767–1855)

The Duke of Reichstadt as a boy

This striking picture demonstrates the versatility of Isabey's talent, for it is far removed from the cool, spare Neoclassicism of his *Self-Portrait* (*see* Plate 21). The Duke is shown playing with a cup-and-ball yet his childhood is simultaneously negated by symbols of his high birth and military destiny: the uniform, sword and drum. Isabey has chosen to frame this composition with the dense undergrowth of a garden, accenting the domesticity of the scene by including a rake, trowel and cut roses, implying that his mother is not far away. Beyond a central image which now strikes us as charming but perhaps somewhat sentimental, the effect of light filtering through the foliage in the background is an astounding technical feat on such a small scale.

PLATE 23

George Chinnery (1774–1852)

Unknown Older Woman

Like many artists in that restless age, Chinnery went abroad after a promising start in London. He moved to Ireland for eight years and then to India, where he stayed for a quarter of a century, until, one step ahead of his creditors, he fled to Macao, where he died. Not chiefly a miniaturist, he was a prolific and various artist in oils, watercolour, and pencil. Like most of his generation Chinnery's chief early influence was Richard Cosway, and this brilliant little portrait is worthy of Cosway himself. Typical of Chinnery is the delicate 'washed' sky. Indeed, some of his miniatures resemble ink-and-wash watercolour sketches – of a very high quality – rather than the traditional 'invisible' bodycolour technique. Here, however, the figure is handled superbly well in the traditional manner, the crisp white folds and frills, pallid skin tone, soft grey hair and blue-ribboned bonnet giving the picture and air of gaiety belied by the sitter's expression.

PLATE 24

Leon Larue (1785 – *c.* 1834)

A Lady, called Mrs Mills

Larue, the son of a painter, came from Nancy, and was a pupil of Isabey. He became one of the leading French miniaturists of the 'second generation' which followed Isabey, Augustin and Guérin in the early nineteenth century. The austerity of the Neo-Classical style has given way here to a richly coloured, densely textured surface, very glossy and superbly finished. The accent is on a sumptuous overall effect, concentrating on the rendition of satins and furs; the sitter was more usually a rich bourgeoise, as here, than an aristocrat. The heavy velvet swathe across the back, and the glimpse of the base of a pillar, are typical of Larue's output, but he was also adept at suggesting a distant, Italianate landscape in many of his works, which gives them a curious but refreshing Renaissance flavour.

A consummate technician, Larue (also known as Mansion) published a treatise on the art of miniature painting in English in 1822. He also spent some time in England and exhibited at the Royal Academy. He seems to have died in middle-age, and represents the last flourish in a rich, jewel-studded tradition.

PLATE 25

Henry Charles Heath (1829–98)

Arthur Sannox Johnston, aged 12

In the second half of the nineteenth century, miniature painting came under increasing commercial pressure from photography. In its earliest years, this was often deliberately contrived to resemble painted art, though was of course far less expensive to produce. For some time, however, the rival forms enjoyed a kind of interdependence, exemplified by the work of H C Heath. Probably trained as an engraver by his father, a leading practitioner, Heath became interested in photography around 1850, but also studied painting.

In the Royal Collection at Windsor are several examples of Heath miniatures which have been painted over photographs imprinted on ivory. Evidently the idea was to combine the complete likeness of photography with the 'finesse' of the miniature. Later, however, Heath concentrated on miniature painting proper, and was a founder of the Society which represents miniaturists to this day. It is perhaps possible, in the case of this picture, to detect the influence, if not the presence of photography, in the very naturalistic and complex rendition of the boy's hair.

PICTURE ACKNOWLEDGEMENTS

The author and publishers would like to thank the following collectors, galleries and photographic libraries for permission to reproduce their illustrations:

COVER
Courtesy of the Trustees of the Victoria & Albert Museum, London (Bridgeman Art Library, London)

INTRODUCTION
Frontispiece: Courtesy of the Board of Trustees of the Victoria & Albert Museum, London (Bridgeman Art Library)
Stadelsches Kunstinstitut, Frankfurt (Bridgeman Art Library)
Courtesy of the Board of Trustees of the Victoria & Albert Museum, London (Bridgeman Art Library)
Courtesy of the Board of Trustees of the Victoria & Albert Museum, London (Bridgeman Art Library)
British Museum, London

PLATES
1 Fitzwilliam Museum, Cambridge (Bridgeman Art Library)
2 Courtesy of the Board of Trustees of the Victoria & Albert Museum, London
3 Courtesy of the National Portrait Gallery, London
4 National Maritime Museum, London (Bridgeman Art Library)
5 Courtesy of the Board of Trustees of the Victoria & Albert Museum, London (Bridgeman Art Library)
6 Courtesy of the Board of Trustees of the Victoria & Albert Museum, London
7 Beauchamp Collection, Madresfield Court (Bridgeman Art Library)
8 Courtesy of the Board of Trustees of the Victoria & Albert Museum, London (Bridgeman Art Library)
9 Courtesy of the Board of Trustees of the Victoria & Albert Museum, London (Bridgeman Art Library)
10 The Royal Collection © 1994 Her Majesty Queen Elizabeth II
11 Courtesy of the Board of Trustees of the Victoria & Albert Museum, London (Bridgeman Art Library)
12 Private Collection (Bridgeman Art Library)
13 Private Collection (Bridgeman Art Library)
14 Courtesy of the Board of Trustees of the Victoria & Albert Museum, London (Bridgeman Art Library)
15 Courtesy of the Board of Trustees of the Victoria & Albert Museum, London
16 Courtesy of the Board of Trustees of the Victoria & Albert Museum, London (Bridgeman Art Library)
17 Courtesy of the Board of Trustees of the Victoria & Albert Museum, London (Bridgeman Art Library)
18 Christie's, London
19 Courtesy of the Board of Trustees of the Victoria & Albert Museum, London (Bridgeman Art Library)
20 By permission of the Trustees of The Wallace Collection, London
21 Courtesy of the Board of Trustees of the Victoria & Albert Museum, London
22 By permission of the Trustees of The Wallace Collection, London
23 Courtesy of the Board of Trustees of the Victoria & Albert Museum, London
24 By permission of the Trustees of The Wallace Collection, London
25 Courtesy of the Board of Trustees of the Victoria & Albert Museum, London